Worry

Pursuing a Better Path to Peace

Resources for Changing Lives

A Ministry of
The Christian Counseling and
Educational Foundation
Glenside, Pennsylvania

RCL Ministry Booklets
Susan Lutz, Series Editor

Worry

Pursuing a Better Path to Peace

David Powlison

P&R
P U B L I S H I N G
P.O. BOX 817 • PHILLIPSBURG • NEW JERSEY 08865-0817

Italics within Scripture quotations indicate emphasis added.

Printed in the United States of America

Library of Congress Cataloging-in-Publication Data

Powlison, David, 1949–
Worry : pursuing a better path to peace / David Powlison.
p. cm.—(Resources for changing lives)
ISBN 0-87552-696-9 (pbk.)
1. Worry—Religious aspects—Christianity. 2. Peace—Religious aspects—Christianity. I. Title. II. Series

BV4908.5.P69 2004
248.8'6—dc22

2003065955

And [Jesus] said to His disciples,

"For this reason I say to you, do not worry about your life, as to what you will eat; nor for your body, as to what you will put on.

"For life is more than food, and the body more than clothing.

"Consider the ravens, for they neither sow nor reap; they have no storeroom nor barn, and yet God feeds them; how much more valuable you are than the birds!

"And which of you by worrying can add a single hour to his life's span?

"If then you cannot do even a very little thing, why do you worry about other matters?

"Consider the lilies, how they grow: they neither toil nor spin; but I tell you, not even Solomon in all his glory clothed himself like one of these.

"But if God so clothes the grass in the field, which is alive today and tomorrow is thrown into the furnace, how much more will He clothe you? You men of little faith!

"And do not seek what you will eat and what you will drink, and do not keep worrying.

"For all these things the nations of the world eagerly seek; but your Father knows that you need these things.

"But seek His kingdom, and these things will be added to you.

"Do not be afraid, little flock, for your Father has chosen gladly to give you the kingdom.

"Sell your possessions and give to charity; make yourselves money belts which do not wear out, an unfailing treasure in heaven, where no thief comes near nor moth destroys.

"For where your treasure is, there your heart will be also."

—Luke 12:22–34

Jesus is talking to a huge crowd out in the open air, on a hillside overlooking the Sea of Galilee. The crowd is mostly simple people: dirt farmers, fishermen, and peasant women. Jesus has been talking to them about two things: who they're most afraid of—God or other people—and their attitude toward him.

Somebody had just interrupted him: "Jesus, Master, tell my brother to give me half of the inheritance! I want my share. I want what's fair" (see Luke 12:13). Jesus cuts the man off and essentially says, "I'm not going to divide inheritances for you. I've got a different plan." But since the man's interruption has turned the conversation to money and possessions, Jesus turns to the crowd and says, "Look out for every form of greed. What you are is not what you own." Money is an issue that reveals a lot about what people most fear, and about how they view Jesus.[1]

Jesus then tells a story about a man who had lots of money (12:16–21). He lived a comfortable life and thought he had no worries. But God said to that man, "You fool! You're going to die tonight. Who's going to have what you worked for your whole life? You have nothing. Your life is an utter waste."

Jesus weaves a warning through the whole story: "Keep your life from every form of greed" (see v. 15). That theme runs through the earlier section (vv. 13–21) right to verse 22: "Keep your life free from *every* form of greed, from the selfish 'I want mine' form of greed, and even from the complacent 'Because I *have* mine, I can sit back and coast' form."

1 Many biblical quotations in this book are the author's paraphrase.

Jesus pursues this topic as he talks straight to the disciples—his friends, the people who love and know him.

"For this reason I say to you, don't worry about your life, as to what you will eat." He's saying that even if you *don't have* a lot of money, or as much as you think you need, money is still not your life. So don't get anxious. Money can't make or break you. Remember that Jesus is talking in a subsistence culture: scratch-plow farmers, poor fishermen, people selling a few items in the marketplace—like a third-world village. Many of us in the United States take food and clothing for granted, but we worry about money too. Although our situations are different, the same issues, attitudes, and temptations play out. "Your life is more than food. Your life is more than money."

Jesus lists reason after reason why you should not be in the grip of fear and worry. First, he says, "Consider the ravens." As Jesus is talking out in the open in Palestine, crows are flying overhead or hopping on the ground squabbling. "Take a look at those crows! They neither sow nor reap. They make no preparations and have no barns. Yet God feeds them. How much more valuable are you than birds?"

He adds a second reason: "Which of you by

worrying can add a single hour to his lifespan? If you can't do the littlest thing like this, why do you worry about the rest?"

Jesus keeps piling on the reasons: "Consider the lilies." He's talking about the kind of tough wildflower that grows in a vacant lot or on the roadside among the weeds. "Look at those flowers over there, how they're growing. They neither toil nor spin"—they make no effort to look pretty. "But I tell you even Solomon in all his glory was not clothed like one of these. If God so clothes the grass of the field, which is alive today and tomorrow is thrown into the furnace, how much more will he clothe you, you of little faith?"

Then Jesus gives a fourth reason. It deals not so much with *feelings* of anxiety as with what you are *living for*. Jesus describes that driven, obsessed preoccupation with money and possessions. "Don't seek what you are going to eat and drink, and don't keep worrying." Of course we should have jobs and make money. But he warns against making it your life objective. "All these things the nations of the world eagerly seek." In other words, that's what everyone in the world is into. But that's their business. "Your Father knows that you need these things. But seek his kingdom.

These things will be added to you." God says, don't live for the one thing everybody else lives for. I'm going to give you something better—and along the way I will take care of you financially.

Lest we should doubt ("Is he *really* going to give something better?"), Jesus gives his next reason. He says, "Don't be afraid, little flock." It's the only place in the Bible where that phrase, "little flock," is used. It's a vivid picture of a flock of sheep small enough that the shepherd knows all their names, their personalities, and what each one faces. Jesus makes sure we know that God is not reluctant to love us. Do not worry, because "Your Father has gladly chosen to give you the kingdom."

Jesus has piled up reasons not to get hung up on money, even when survival is at stake. This leads to radical implications for your lifestyle. "Sell your possessions, give to charity." Instead of being characterized by every form of greed, where we say, "What's in it for me? I want my share! I've got a lot, so I can sit comfortably! What if I don't have enough? Maybe I won't get something I need!"—instead of all that, *you can give because you have been given to*. Why? Because your Father who loves you gives you a life that you can give away and not lose. "Make yourselves money belts that don't wear out—store up that unfailing treasure in heaven where no thief comes and no moth destroys. Where your treasure is your heart will be also."

You've Got Plenty of Good Reasons to Worry!

We need these strong and comforting words, because we do have good reasons to worry. Take the people Jesus is talking to. They are *poor* people with primitive sanitation and no health care. When drought comes, they die.

This passage shows us that we all worry about many things. We all get obsessed about the wrong things. If you are six years old, perhaps it comes in at this level: "My older brother gets three dollars more for his allowance. If only I had that extra three dollars." If you're the ten-year-old brother, you think, "My sister is so lucky, because she has a job. If only I had a job!" Then you get a job—which you think will solve all your worries. But now you've got bills, and everything you want costs more.

Let's say you have that after-school job and can put some money in your pocket. You still worry. "How will I pay for college? What kind of a part-time job or student loan will I need?" If you're in college or just graduating, you worry, "Will I get a decent job? What if there's no work?" When you get that real job, "Will I ever have enough money for a house? How are we going to afford kids?" There are always more reasons to worry. Does all this sound familiar? Even when I have enough money to pay all the bills, I leave my bill-paying sessions with a vague anxiety. After I've paid everything, there's not much money left. Low-grade worry sneaks in. In my budget it's always the dentist or the auto mechanic. It was never in my budget, but it easily gets onto my worry list.

Then you get older and start doing financial planning for retirement—which you should have been thinking about twenty years before (another worry). The planners show you diagrams of your projected assets. The amount goes up for a little while, and then takes a nosedive at age seventy-five. You're better off dying before you're eighty-two—or you'll be in the poorhouse or dependent on your kids. Then there's your 401K: the stock market crashes. . . .

There's *always* something to worry about.

One of the things that makes money such a

powerful source of worry is its obsessive component. It's always there. It says "Goodnight" and wakes you up in the middle of the night. It greets you in the morning with, "Hi, here I am. Think about me." Financial worries play with your mind, and all the other worries operate in exactly the same way. What you see in common with all of them is that they are *uncertain*. We ask, "Am I going to get that? Maybe, maybe not. If I have it, could I lose it? Maybe, maybe not." We worry about things that are inherently uncertain. You can never be sure. Money is a great example, but what other things plague you? What are the one, two, six, dozen things that you tend to worry about? Do you find yourself dwelling on any of the following?

- "Do I have any real friends?"
- "What if I don't make the team? What if I forget my lines in the play? What if someone else gets picked for that committee?
- "Will I ever find a spouse?"
- "If I do find one, will he or she be faithful?"
- "Am I worth marrying?"
- "Will I be able to have kids?"
- "If I have kids, how will they turn out?"
- "What about my health? Some of my friends are dying of cancer. Is that going to

be me? What if I get Alzheimer's and die unable even to recognize the people I love?"

Worry rages about your health, your money, your relationships, and your achievements. Any of those things can hijack the controls of your mind. The fact is, you can't control any of them. There is every reason in the world to worry about them. So ask yourself: What do *you* worry about?

But there's a second question to ask yourself: When all is said and done, *why* do you worry? Why do you fret about these things in the first place? Why do you get preoccupied, or driven, or have panic attacks, or brood, or whatever form your anxiety takes?

The easy answer is to point your finger at *what* you are worrying about, as if that explains it. "I'm worried because I don't know if I'm going to get a job. I'm worried because I don't have enough saved for retirement. I'm worried because I have a family history of cancer." But Jesus doesn't allow that. He explains our worries not by pointing to how uncertain life is, but by pointing to something *in us*. Throughout this passage he says, "You worry because of *you*, not because of *things*." That's why he said "Guard *yourself* from every form of greed."

"I want my share of what's fair" was one form of greed. *Covetous* greed will make you angry and manipulative. You'll even break in to interrupt Jesus when he's talking!

"I am set. I can kick back. I've got plenty!" That was a different form of greed. *Complacent, satisfied* greed makes you care less about what really matters, because it lulls you to sleep.

In this passage, where Jesus is talking to his disciples about not being anxious, he goes after a third form of greed. "What if I don't have enough? What if what I need isn't there?" That's *anxious* greed. I want something I might not get, so I worry.

Later in the passage Jesus captures the same thing from a different angle: "O you of little faith!" Little faith does not mean *no* faith. Rather, it's like a flashlight with drained batteries. It still makes light, but the light is flickering and uncertain. The faith is dying out. We lose sight of God because what we want (and worry about) is the only thing we see. Jesus helps us to spot things: "Where do I go off? What makes me forget? Why do I fret? Why do I lose it?" When faith is dying out, greed and worry come to life.

The middle of the passage offers another reason why you worry. "Which of you by worrying can add a single cubit to his lifespan, a single hour? If you can't even do a small thing, why are you worrying about the rest?" Worriers act as if they might be able to control the uncontrollable. Central to worry is the illusion that we can *control* things. "If only I could get my retirement right, I could control the future." "If I could get my diet and medicine right, I wouldn't get cancer." "If I could figure out the right childrearing technique, I could guarantee how my kids turn out." Worry assumes the possibility of control over the uncontrollable. The illusion of control lurks inside your anxiety. Anxiety and control are two sides of one coin. When we can't control something, we worry about it.

Jesus' final comment offers one more reason *why* you worry. A worrier is storing "treasure" in the wrong place. If what you *most value* can be taken away or destroyed, then you set yourself up for anxiety. Whether it be money, health, a particular friendship, the dream of marriage, success in sports or business, or how your children turn out, you're building your house on sand. Even if you feel good or everything's going your way, you're building your house on sand. Your treasure is vulnerable. And whenever what is "precious" to you is threatened, you'll be gripped with fear. Where do y your treasure? In iffy things or certainties.

So why do *you* worry? What life objectives snuff out your awareness of God? What makes you want to control your world? Understand those things, and Jesus' alternative will become very, very precious to you.

You've Got Better Reasons *Not* to Worry!

Jesus has no interest in simply talking about what's wrong with us. He's always going somewhere good. He does make reference to our temptations and failures, but he's more concerned with giving you solid reasons not to worry. Yes, you have reason to worry because things are uncertain. But you have many, much better reasons *not* to worry!

Some things are *certain!*

Jesus lays them out for his disciples, wooing, informing, and encouraging them. Be persuaded and heartened as you read. "Don't worry" doesn't hang in space as a moral platitude! Jesus gives you solid reasons to live without fretting—even when you're facing the very things that are inherently uncertain and uncontrollable.

Below are seven promises Jesus makes,

seven reasons for you not to worry. Which one do *you* find most inviting? Which one is most necessary and helpful, where you can say, "If I remember _________, I'll be a different person this week. I would not worry about money, health, friends, whatever"? Which of these *better* reasons do you most need?

1. Your life is so much more than food or clothing. There's so much more to who you are than what you have or don't have. Jesus refers back to the story of the rich fool whose money couldn't give him identity or meaning or security or life. Therefore, Jesus adds, "If your life isn't *made* by having money, then your life can't be *unmade* by the lack of it!" What matters a lot more is "Whom do you fear?" and "What do you do with Jesus?" Those are matters of life and death.

Everyone knows people who are living for empty, foolish things. The twenty-three-year-old woman who is living to be beautiful will only find that she will grow old and wrinkly. It's a losing bet from the start.

Those who live for health or athleticism or adventures inevitably start to get knee injuries after age thirty-five. Reflexes slow down. Systems start to break down. Sooner or later, death surely comes. It's foolish! There is more to life than health and sports and vacations!

It's like that with everything we live for—and worry about. If you live for money, you are banking on a clunker. The "car" is a lemon; it will *always* break down and give you reason to worry. There are better things to give your energies to. There is something much more important going on in your life than the stuff you worry about. Go through your worry list one by one. Jesus promises, "Your life is more than __________." That's promise Number 1.

2. Jesus tells people to look around at the world. In this case, *look at crows*. Jesus says, "Consider the ravens. God feeds them even though they don't put a single seed in the ground. They don't ever water their crops. They don't store a thing for next year—not even for tomorrow. They live in the moment, but God provides for them."

How does God feed them? It's not romantic in the least. A crow is a scavenger. They are dirty, tough, aggressive, and smart. They are noisy, obnoxious pests. How does God feed crows? Road kill. Trash picking. Raiding your crops. That's why you have scarecrows. God feeds the crows as they steal your food and pick over your garbage!

God's provision for the crows came home vividly to me one summer. A treasured plum tree grows in our yard. That year it was the only one of our five fruit trees to bear fruit. As summer unfolded, no less than forty, beautiful, sweet plums (I counted them!) were coming to ripeness. I couldn't wait!

One day when I came home, there were only twenty plums left on the tree. A gang of crows was having a feast on *my* precious plums! Earlier in the year this gang of six crows had moved into our neighborhood. I called them the Crow Boys. They made all kinds of racket early in the morning and they were always scavenging. And the Crow Boys had found *my* plum tree. I was not happy. We had planted this tree as a family. I prune it regularly and spray it faithfully. I had been eagerly looking forward to those forty juicy plums. And now there were only twenty left.

I mobilized our defenses. I threw ice cubes at the crows, banged trash cans, and ran to buy netting to put over the tree. By the time I got back, there were only twelve plums left on the tree. I draped the netting. When any crow tried to land, he would get a big, unpleasant surprise. Sure enough, a few minutes later, the first crow swooped in. He hit the netting, got tangled and flustered, and flapped off irritably, "Caw! Caw! Caw! Caw!" So I thought, *Maybe I've won!*

But by the end of that day, there were *zero* plums left on my tree! Those crows were too smart. They had figured out how to come up from the bottom of the tree. They would land on the ground, and hop up through the branches close to the trunk where the netting didn't reach. They cleaned me out!

God's sense of timing and sense of humor are very interesting: quite a "coincidence" that I had to preach on this passage a month later. Jesus says to me, "Oh, David, by the way, look how God provides for the crows." Yes, he provides by using *my* fruit trees! But here's the promise: *You are much more important than crows*. Yes, the scavengers get fed. But how much more does God care about you? Do you see what Jesus is saying here? God feeds a bird, even one of the Old Testament's unclean animals, a bird that lives on road kill and theft. People matter a *lot* more to God. That's a promise you can take home.

3. Which of you by worrying can add a single hour to his life? Literally, Jesus says, "Which of you by worrying can add a cubit to his span?" A cubit is a distance measure: eighteen inches, your elbow to your fingers. The Bible envisions life as a "walk." You walk through your life, step by step. Jesus is saying, "You won't get even eighteen inches further by worrying. You can't even get half a step further by worrying." Worrying does . . . nothing. It accomplishes . . . zero. It won't get you eighteen inches further down the path of your life.

4. *"Consider the lilies of the field, how they grow.* They neither toil nor spin, yet I say unto you that even Solomon in all his glory is not clothed like one of these." Again, Jesus is pointing to weed flowers growing in vacant lots. The flowers that grow on their own are beautiful, without any tending or care except God's. Jesus starts with the same logic as with the crows: Look at something familiar—but he ups the ante this time. If God makes mere wildflowers so glorious that their beauty outdazzles Solomon, how much more will *you* outdazzle the lilies, O you of little faith! This promise is *far* more than "God will take care of you." This is "God will clothe you in nothing less than his radiant glory!" "So why do you worry about the clothes you wear? I'll dress you in my own glory! Why do you worry about your health? I'll raise you from the dead to eternal life. Why do you worry about a few dollars? I'll give you the whole earth as your inheritance. Why do you worry when someone doesn't like you? I'll make you live in the kingdom of my love!"

This fourth promise, rightly understood, is a spectacular reason not to worry. God is giving you a life that is radiant, indestructible, and full of glory. You will *dazzle*. If God so adorns mere wildflowers with glory, how much more will he make you as radiant as himself!

5. "Don't seek what you are going to eat and drink. Don't keep worrying about these things"—the word for worry here means more than feeling anxious; it means to be obsessed, driven, preoccupied—"All these things the nations of the world eagerly seek." We could put it this way: *Look at what everybody everywhere is after*. Are you going to march in step with the crowd just because everybody else does it?

Take, for example, the Sunday newspaper. What percentage of it is about money? Ninety percent? It's not just the business and financial sections. Look at the automobile section, the housing section, the want ads, the jobs, the coupons, and all the other advertising. Most of the news articles—covering wars, crime, budgets, taxes—are also about money. Even the sports section dwells on possible strikes and salaries. The newspaper covers what everyone is into—and it's ninety percent money.

So life is about money, according to the Sunday paper. That's what counts as news. That's what people are interested in. But what about the Bible? It talks a lot about money—maybe five percent is directly about money and property. But the Bible is one hundred percent about what *really* matters. It asks, "What is your attitude toward money? People live for *either* God *or* money—what will it be for you?" The Bible is about what really lasts, what's certain. It's about the living God, the One who made us in his image, who made us to live our lives for something bigger and better than the things we tend to worry about and define our lives by.

Yes, we do have economic needs. Jesus says, "I promise you, your Father knows you need these things." You do need a job. It's not wrong to provide for retirement, to pay your mortgage and bills, to own a car. Your Father knows you need these. But what are you going to be *about?* Is your life *about* money? Everyone else's life is: "The nations of the world *eagerly seek* these things." Jesus says, "Your Father will give what you need." If you just get the *big* things straightened out, you will have what you need in the little things. What everyone in the world is obsessed with, God makes a distant second. He'll give you what you need to live on if you *need* him in order to live.

6. God promises you . . . himself. Jesus keeps giving better reason after better reason. His sixth promise is the most significant of all. Some of what Jesus has been saying might sink in by reading the paper, looking at crows, looking at flowers, or thinking a minute about how useless it is to worry. It *is* God's world, so life works the way he says it does. But you'd never see how *God* connects to the crows or the flowers unless he tells you. This sixth reason is the capstone, the climax of Jesus' argument. In effect what Jesus says is, *your Father* knows you need these things. If you are preoccupied with *his kingdom*, then the other things you need will be added on. Get your life to be about what *your Father* is about.

This promise directly meets our tendency toward anxiety. We know what happens if we live for money, health, being pretty, having a boyfriend or girlfriend, or job success. But what guarantee do you have that Jesus' kingdom won't turn out to be one more iffy bet, one more disappointment? Jesus firmly and tenderly emphasizes this promise: "*Your Father knows what you need.* . . . Don't be afraid, *little flock*, because *your Father has chosen gladly to give*. . . ." You can rest on this. Jesus makes it as personal, intimate, and generous as possible. He wants you to really understand this, to stake your life on this and never be disappointed. As we said earlier, the shepherd of a "little flock" knows every single sheep by name. He knows everything about you, and it is his *pleasure* to give you the kingdom. He invites you, "Leave your anxious fretting, and seek my kingdom." We could say a hundred things about what that kingdom means.

I once talked with a close friend who described a series of painful experiences. She had become very discouraged, doing a lot of worrying, brooding, and floundering. She couldn't get traction in her life. She felt swept away by tension and confusion. She was seeking God, but couldn't seem to find him. Then, like a bolt of lightning, the thought came into her mind, "Your father . . . is *God*. Your father is God." She described how her worries changed. The circumstances didn't go away: the child's disability, the husband's financial problems, uncertainties about her health, conflicts in her extended family, and miserable things from her past still lingered. But the promise weighed more: "Your father . . . is God." That supreme and simple promise came in and rearranged how she saw life and what she lived for. It drained the life from her worrying. You can say, "My father is God. He is more than willing to give me his kingdom. It is his pleasure. He chooses gladly to love me." One of the things the kingdom means to you is, "My father is God."

I once watched a toddler wade into the shallow end of the baby pool. She headed boldly toward the deep end, without fear. She started out—ankle deep, up to her knees, then to her waist. Pretty soon the water was up to shoulder level. She kept heading into the deep end. What if she stumbled? She wasn't all that stable on her feet yet. But right behind her walked her mom, with arms outstretched, two alert hands poised inches from the little girl's shoulders. At one point the girl slipped slightly. I don't think she even realized it, but her mother reached out and steadied her. "Your father is God." Someone is right there, like that mom with her toddler.

What else does it look like to be given the

kingdom? It's being able to say Psalm 121: "My helper is the LORD who made heaven and earth." Or meditate on this: "My rescuer is the Messiah of the world, Jesus." Or, "My Savior, who bears the substitutionary sacrifice, is the Lamb of God, the one good man, the only Savior of the world."

Or say, "My shepherd is the LORD. I shall not want. Why would I be afraid? What am I so uptight about?" If life is like the entire electromagnetic spectrum, from infrared to ultraviolet with every wavelength in between, why do we obsess and fret, as if all of life were found in the green band, the money band? Money is part of life, but wake up! Your Father is concerned with the entire spectrum. It is his pleasure to give you the kingdom, little flock, beloved children.

7. Having given you so much, your Father calls you to the radical freedom of giving your life away. It's both a reason and an alternative. Everything before was *get*. We become anxious because we want to *get*. We don't want to lose what we've *got*. We become presumptuous, and kick back into a life of leisure, because we have *gotten*. Everything is get, got, gotten. But the end of Jesus' message is all *give*. Because you have been given a sure thing, because there's nothing to really worry about, then *give*. It's his pleasure to give to you, so you can give, too. When that sinks in, a marvelous transformation takes place. You have good reasons to let your worries go. We—who tend to be obsessed and anxious about money—become able to open our hands.

Jesus says, "Sell your possessions, give alms." That doesn't mean you have to live exactly like Francis of Assisi—but to have Francis of Assisi's attitude. In that is the only true freedom and the only real happiness. It's an attitude of trusting your Father and living a life that's worth something. You can give yourself away. You can use your gifts. Your life can be about *give*. There's a world to reach out to, and people to love, and jobs to be done, and we can give ourselves to that purpose. Your Father knows what you need. He promises to provide for you, as needed. But get first things first. Live for the kingdom. When you do, it works directly against the uncertainty of the things we worry about.

Jesus describes this kingdom investment as "money belts that do not wear out." You can own something that will never get old. It will never wear out or run out. An unfailing treasure. You can live for and give away something that is inexhaustible. Yes, that crash in the retirement income means your assets might get exhausted. But here's a treasure that's inexhaustible. The spring is always flowing. Nothing and no one can ever take it away from you. This "purse" can never get stolen or motheaten or useless or lost.

Jesus says, "I promise you, the best thing you could ever want you will never lose." This is an amazing truth! All the things we worry about are what we want but could lose. That's why we worry. The best thing you could ever want you will never lose, and you can always give it away. "If you die for me, you will live"—that's a promise. It's the fundamental way redemption works. If you die for Christ, you will live. Your Father will provide, so you can give generously.

Fending Off the Barbarians in Your Mind

Proverbs 25:28 offers a good description of what happens with anxiety. "Like a city that is broken into and without walls is a man who has no control over his spirit." How do you get a grip when barbarians are rioting in the streets of your mind? Fear and anxiety have taken over. Nothing is safe or certain.

Anxiety is a universal human experience, and you need to approach it with a plan. A plan is not a formula. A football coach doesn't know a single thing that's going to happen after the opening whistle. He doesn't even know who's going to kick off until they flip a coin. But he's not unprepared. He goes in with a *game plan*, a basic orientation to the game ahead. Here are six things to use as a game plan when you start to worry and obsess.

1. *Name the pressures*. You always worry about *something*. What things tend to hook you? What "good reasons" do you have for anxiety? The very act of naming it is often helpful. In the midst of the experience of anxiety, it seems as if a million things are overwhelming you. You're juggling plates, round and round and round. But really, you're juggling only six plates—or maybe obsessing on just one. It helps to name the one thing or the six that keep recycling. Anxieties feel endless and infinite—but they're finite and specific.
2. *Identify how you express anxiety*. How does anxiety show up in your life? For some people it's the feeling of panic clutching

their throat, or just a vague uneasiness. For others it's repetitive, obsessive thoughts: "Oh, now that's the fourth time I've repeated that scenario in my mind." For some people the sign is anger. They get irritated, but when they work back, they realize, "I was fearful and worried about something." For other people, worry shows up in their bodies (e.g., a tension headache) or in the cheap remedies that sin manufactures to make us feel better (e.g., gobbling ice cream, or an overpowering desire for a stiff drink). Identify the signs. How can they become cues to you? "I'm losing it, I'm forgetting God, my flashlight is going dim."

3. *Ask yourself, Why am I anxious?* Worry always has its inner logic. Anxious people are "you of little faith." If I've forgotten God, who or what has started to rule in his place? Identify the hijacker. Anxious people have fallen into one of the subsets of "every form of greed." What do I want, need, crave, expect, demand, and lust after? Or what do I fear either losing or never getting? Identify the specific lust of the flesh. Anxious people "eagerly seek" the gifts more than the Giver. They bank

treasure in the wrong place. What is preoccupying me, so that I pursue it with all my heart? Identify the object of your affections.

4. *Which promise of Jesus speaks to you most?* Take to heart those seven promises. They are all good reasons. But it's tough to remember seven things at once, so pick one. For some time, the most helpful to me was, "If God feeds the crows, won't he provide for you?" It made me laugh even to think about it. Those Crow Boys intercepted a lot of temptations to anxiety. They did me good. Grab one promise and work with it.
5. *Go to your Father*. Talk to him. Your Father cares about the things you worry about. *Your Father* knows what you need. Cast your cares on him, because he cares for you. You'll have to leave your worries with him—they are *always* outside of your control! How will your kids turn out? Will you get Alzheimer's? What will happen with the economy? Will your dad come to know the Lord? You have good reasons to be concerned about such things, but you have better reasons to take them to Someone who loves you. Like that tod-

dler whose mom trailed her, even the deep end of life is safe.

6. *Give*. Do and say something constructive. Care for someone else. Give to meet human need. In the darkest hole, when life is toughest, there's always some way to give yourself away. The problem might seem overwhelming. You could worry, worry, worry. But what you're called to do is just a small thing. There's always something to give yourself to, and some way to give. Jesus said more about this in Matthew 6, a parallel passage: "Let the day's own trouble be sufficient for the day thereof." Give yourself to today's trouble. Leave tomorrow's uncertainties to your Father.

It is *your Father's pleasure* to give you the kingdom. Your father is God. Don't worry.

David Powlison *is the editor of* the Journal of Biblical Counseling *and a member of the faculty and counseling staff at the Christian Counseling and Educational Foundation in Glenside, Pennsylvania.*

RCL Ministry Booklets

A.D.D.: Wandering Minds and Wired Bodies, by Edward T. Welch

Anger: Escaping the Maze, by David Powlison

Angry at God?: Bring Him Your Doubts and Questions, by Robert D. Jones

Bad Memories: Getting Past Your Past, by Robert D. Jones

Depression: The Way Up When You Are Down, by Edward T. Welch

Domestic Abuse: How to Help, by David Powlison, Paul David Tripp, and Edward T. Welch

Forgiveness: "I Just Can't Forgive Myself!" by Robert D. Jones

God's Love: Better than Unconditional, by David Powlison

Guidance: Have I Missed God's Best? by James C. Petty

Homosexuality: Speaking the Truth in Love, by Edward T. Welch

"Just One More": When Desires Don't Take No for an Answer, by Edward T. Welch

Marriage: Whose Dream? by Paul David Tripp

Motives: "Why Do I Do the Things I Do?" by Edward T. Welch

OCD: Freedom for the Obsessive-Compulsive, by Michael R. Emlet

Pornography: Slaying the Dragon, by David Powlison

Pre-Engagement: 5 Questions to Ask Yourselves, by David Powlison and John Yenchko

Priorities: Mastering Time Management, by James C. Petty

Procrastination: First Steps to Change, by Walter Henegar

Self-Injury: When Pain Feels Good, by Edward T. Welch

Sexual Sin: Combatting the Drifting and Cheating, by Jeffrey S. Black

Stress: Peace amid Pressure, by David Powlison

Suffering: Eternity Makes a Difference, by Paul David Tripp

Suicide: Understanding and Intervening, by Jeffrey S. Black

Teens and Sex: How Should We Teach Them? by Paul David Tripp

Thankfulness: Even When It Hurts, by Susan Lutz

Why Me?: Comfort for the Victimized, by David Powlison

Worry: Pursuing a Better Path to Peace, by David Powlison